WHY AM I LIKE THIS?

How to leave yesterday,

accept today and

face tomorrow

John Salyer

Table of Content

Chapter One
The truth about your past failures
Chapter Two
Identity crisis : How to discover and love yourself
Chapter Three
Negative mindset: A cage
Chapter Four
How long it takes to change

Chapter One

The truth about your past failures

It's a period for learning

Failing can be a great teacher, teaching us to keep going despite setbacks and become more resilient. It can also help us to identify what went wrong and refine our strategies.

Failure can humble us, reminding us that no one is perfect and that there is always room for improvement. It can also force us to find alternative paths, encouraging creativity and innovation. Facing failure and continuing to pursue our goals shows determination and perseverance. It can also help us to assess risks and plan more effectively. Experiencing failure can make us more understanding and compassionate towards others who are going through similar challenges. It can also make eventual successes more rewarding and meaningful. Confronting failure can reduce our fear of it, allowing us to take calculated risks in the future. Finally, it can encourage introspection, helping us to identify our strengths, weaknesses, and areas for growth.

Bad experiences can also be a great teacher, if you choose to learn from them. Self-awareness, boundaries, red flags, problem-solving, empathy, personal growth, adaptability, perspective, appreciation, and resilience are all valuable lessons that can be gained from difficult times. By reflecting on these experiences, you can gain a better understanding of yourself, set healthier boundaries, recognize warning signs, develop problem-solving skills, become more empathetic, grow personally, become more adaptable, gain a new perspective, appreciate the positive aspects of life, and build resilience. Remember, the value of bad experiences lies in what you choose to learn and how you apply those lessons moving forward.

Emotional impact of failure

Failing to reach a goal can be a huge letdown, and it can bring up a range of emotions. Disappointment, frustration, guilt, regret, shame, sadness, anxiety, low self-esteem, stress, isolation, and a lack of motivation are all common reactions to failure. It's important to handle these feelings in a healthy way. Talking to friends, family, or a professional, taking care of yourself, and learning from the experience can help you cope with the emotional impact of failure. With time, these experiences can help you become more emotionally resilient and help you grow.

A qualification for success

Failure can be a great teacher and a qualification for success in many ways. It can help build resilience, teaching you to bounce back from setbacks and keep striving for your goals. It can also help you become more adaptable, allowing you to find alternative paths and navigate challenges more effectively. Mistakes can provide invaluable lessons that you can use to refine your strategies and decision-making in the future. Failing can also humble you, keeping you open to learning and feedback, which are essential for success. It can also make you more willing to take calculated risks, which can lead to innovation and breakthroughs. Overcoming failure can also ignite a strong motivation to prove yourself, driving you to work harder and smarter. It can also present complex problems to solve, enhancing your problem-solving skills and creative thinking. It can also foster a deeper appreciation for the process, highlighting the importance of consistent effort and patience. Experiencing failure can also make you more empathetic towards others who face similar challenges, enabling better teamwork and leadership. Finally, it can give you a greater appreciation for success when you eventually achieve it, making it more meaningful.

Ultimately, viewing failure as a qualification for success means accepting it as a natural part of growth. It equips you with skills, perspectives, and qualities that are essential for reaching your goals and thriving in various aspects of life.

The quality of failure

The quality of failure is not determined by the failure itself, but by how you react and what you learn from it. Here are some aspects that define the quality of failure:

1. Learning: Being willing to take away valuable lessons from your failures, understanding what went wrong and how to improve.

2. Adaptation: Your capacity to adjust your approach and strategies based on the insights gained from failure, showing flexibility.

3. Ownership: Taking responsibility for your mistakes and decisions instead of blaming external factors.

4. Reflection: Engaging in self-reflection to comprehend your emotions, thoughts, and actions related to the failure.

5. Resilience: Recovering from failure with renewed determination and persistence, refusing to be discouraged.

6. Growth Mindset: Seeing failure as an opportunity for growth, embracing challenges as chances to expand your abilities.

7. Risk-Taking: Being ready to take risks even after experiencing failure, exhibiting a willingness to explore uncharted territory.

8. Positive Attitude: Keeping a positive outlook, focusing on solutions rather than dwelling on the negative aspects of failure.

9. Perseverance:Continuing to strive towards your goals despite setbacks, displaying determination and perseverance.

10. Application: Applying the lessons learned from failure to future endeavors, effectively incorporating newfound knowledge.

In a nutshell, the quality of failure is a measure of your response, resilience, and capacity to transform setbacks into stepping stones for personal and professional growth. It's not about avoiding failure, but about using it as a tool for self-improvement and advancement.

How failure can be a powerful tool to help you reach success:

1. Valuable Lessons:Failing can teach you valuable lessons that you wouldn't have learned otherwise, giving you more knowledge and experience.

2. Course Correction: Experiencing failure can help you reevaluate your approach and make the necessary changes, leading you to a more successful path.

3. Resilience Building:Overcoming failure can help you become more resilient, making it easier to handle future challenges and setbacks.

4. Innovation: Failing can push you to think outside the box, resulting in creative solutions and ideas that you may not have thought of before.

5. Motivation: The desire to prove yourself after a failure can be a great motivator, pushing you to work harder and smarter.

6. Character Development:Dealing with failure can help you grow as a person and professionally, testing your character and determination.

7. Realistic Expectations:Failure can help you set more realistic goals, preventing you from having overly optimistic expectations.

8. Risk-Taking: Accepting failure can reduce the fear of taking risks, encouraging you to explore new territories and ideas.

9. Success Appreciation: Failing can make successes even more rewarding, providing a contrasting backdrop that highlights your achievements.

10. Story of Triumph:Turning failure into success can create a powerful story that resonates with others, inspiring them to keep going through their own struggles.

It's not the number of failures you have, but how you interpret and respond to them that will determine your journey to success. Each failure can be a stepping stone, helping you reach your goals with more wisdom and determination.

Chapter Two

Identity crisis : How to discover and love yourself

Know your weakness and strength

Self-reflection and feedback from others can help you to identify your strengths and weaknesses. Think about the things you find difficult, the tasks you tend to avoid, or the areas where you don't feel so confident. These could be your weaknesses. Your strengths, on the other hand, are the things you do well, the activities that give you energy, or the qualities that people admire in you. Ask your friends, family, and colleagues for their opinions, as they can provide you with valuable insights. Keep track of your progress and adjust your approach as you learn more about yourself.

Identifying your weaknesses and strengths is an important step in personal and professional growth. Here are the steps to help you do that:

Identifying Weaknesses:

1. Self-Reflection: Take some time to think about tasks or areas where you have difficulty, feel uncomfortable, or avoid. Also, remember any feedback you have received about areas needing improvement.

2. Feedback: Ask for input from people you trust, such as friends, family, and colleagues. They can provide insights on your weaknesses that you may not be aware of.

3. Challenges: Note down situations that consistently challenge you or make you feel overwhelmed. These could point to areas where you need to improve.

4. Comparison: Compare your skills and abilities with those who excel in similar roles or tasks. Identify gaps where you fall short.

5. Self-Assessment Tools:Use self-assessment tools or personality tests to gain insights into your weaknesses. These tools often provide a structured way to analyze your traits.

Identifying Strengths:

1. Passion and Energy: Think about activities that energize you and bring you joy. These activities are often aligned with your strengths.

2. Natural Talent: Identify tasks that come easily to you without much effort. These tasks are likely related to your strengths.

3. Feedback: Listen to compliments and feedback from others about what you do well. Their observations can give you hints about your strengths.

4. Success Stories: Reflect on moments when you achieved exceptional results or received recognition. These achievements highlight your strengths.

5. Personal Satisfaction: Consider tasks that give you a sense of accomplishment and satisfaction. Your strengths often lie in areas where you excel.

6. Observation:Pay attention to situations where you've been asked for help or guidance. People often seek assistance from those who possess relevant strengths.

Analyzing the Results:

1. Make a List: Create a list of identified weaknesses and strengths based on your self-reflection, feedback, and observations.

2. Prioritize: Prioritize the weaknesses you believe are most critical to address. Similarly, prioritize the strengths that align with your goals.

3. Action Plan:nDevelop an action plan to work on your weaknesses. This could involve seeking training, practicing, or finding ways to overcome challenges.

4. Utilize Strengths: Look for opportunities to use your strengths in your personal and professional life. Look for tasks, roles, or projects that align with what you excel at.

5. Continual Assessment: Regularly reassess your weaknesses and strengths. As you grow and develop, these may change, so it's important to stay self-aware.

Remember that both weaknesses and strengths are important parts of your identity. Embracing both sides and actively working on improvement can lead to personal and professional growth.

Advantages of Weakness and strength

Absolutely! Both weaknesses and strengths have their own benefits: Weaknesses can give you the chance to develop and grow, as well as foster humility and self-awareness. Overcoming challenges related to your weaknesses can be a great learning experience. On the other hand, strengths can give you confidence, help you be more efficient, and make a positive impact on those around you. Additionally, engaging in activities that align with your strengths can be more enjoyable and fulfilling. Finally, your strengths can make you stand out in your personal and professional life. All in all, weaknesses and strengths both have their advantages, and finding a balance between the two can lead to a successful life.

Stop thinking, know yourself

"Take a moment to pause and get to know yourself" is a great reminder of the importance of self-awareness and mindfulness. It suggests that by taking a break from the constant stream of thoughts and turning inward, you can gain a better understanding of who you really are. Here's a bit more about this concept:

1. Mindfulness: This phrase encourages the practice of mindfulness, which involves being present in the moment without judgment. By stopping the never-ending flow of thoughts, you can focus on the present and gain clarity.

2. Self-Reflection: Knowing yourself requires introspection. Taking the time to

reflect on your thoughts, emotions, motivations, and behaviors can lead to greater self-awareness.

3. Authenticity:n Understanding yourself helps you live authentically. When you know your values, strengths, weaknesses, and aspirations, you can make decisions that are true to your true self.

4. Inner Wisdom: Often, the answers to life's questions lie within us. By stopping the noise of external influences and turning inward, you can tap into your inner wisdom and make choices that resonate with you.

5. Growth: Self-awareness is the foundation of personal growth. Recognizing areas of improvement allows you to actively work on them, leading to continuous self-improvement.

6. Emotional Intelligence: Knowing yourself enhances emotional intelligence. You can

better understand your reactions and emotions, leading to improved relationships and communication.

7. Decision-Making: When you understand your core values and desires, decision-making becomes easier. You can make choices that align with your goals and aspirations.

8. Acceptance: Self-awareness involves accepting both your strengths and weaknesses. This acceptance leads to self-compassion and a healthier self-image.

9. Lifelong Journey: Knowing yourself is not a one-time achievement; it's an ongoing journey. As you grow and evolve, your self-awareness deepens, and you gain new insights.

In a world filled with distractions and external influences, taking a moment to pause and get to know yourself can bring about a sense of clarity, purpose, and inner peace. It's a call to connect with your authentic self and make choices that lead to a more fulfilling and meaningful life.

Wakeup to your real identity

"Waking up to your true self" is a powerful reminder to recognize and embrace your authentic identity, beyond the expectations of society or external influences. Here's more about this concept:

1. Unveiling Social Conditioning:Society often imposes roles and expectations on individuals. "Waking up" involves removing these external masks and discovering the real you.

2. Genuineness: Embracing your true identity means being genuine. It's about honoring your values, passions, strengths, and quirks instead of conforming to what others want you to be.

3. Self-Inquiry: To wake up to your real identity, you must explore your inner world. This involves self-reflection, questioning beliefs, and understanding your motivations.

4. Accepting Imperfections: Your real identity isn't about perfection; it's about accepting your imperfections. It's recognizing that flaws are part of what makes you unique.

5. Letting Go: Sometimes, societal pressures lead us to hold onto identities that no longer serve us. "Waking up" involves letting go of identities that no longer resonate with who you are becoming.

6. Self-Love: Discovering your real identity often leads to self-love. You learn to treat yourself with compassion and kindness, nurturing a healthy relationship with yourself.

7. Refraining from Comparison: Waking up to your real identity requires resisting the urge to compare yourself to others. It's recognizing that your journey is uniquely yours.

8. Empowerment: Embracing your true self empowers you to make choices that align with your passions and goals. It's about taking control of your life's direction.

9. Breaking Habits: Sometimes, people adopt identities to fit into specific roles or expectations. Waking up involves breaking free from these patterns and forging your path.

10. Personal Growth: Awakening to your real identity is a journey of personal growth. It involves continuous self-discovery and evolution.

In a world where external influences often shape our perceptions of ourselves, "waking up to your real identity" is a reminder that you have the power to define who you are.

The place for peoples view in knowing

The views and opinions of other people can have a major effect on a person's journey of self-discovery. External perspectives can provide useful insights, helping people to understand themselves better and uncover aspects of their identity that they may not have noticed. Nevertheless, it is important to remember that while others' views can be helpful, they should not be the ones to decide or define one's identity. True self-discovery involves a balance between internal contemplation and external feedback, allowing individuals to explore their identity based on a combination of their own values, experiences, and the input of those around them.

The opinions of others can be a great asset in the journey of self-discovery. They can act as mirrors, reflecting aspects of our personality, behavior, and values that we may not have noticed ourselves. Constructive feedback and observations from friends, family, and colleagues can help us to identify our strengths and weaknesses, as well as areas for improvement.

It is important to approach these viewpoints with a critical yet open-minded attitude. Not all external opinions are accurate or in line with our true selves, as they may be influenced by their own biases, misunderstandings, or limited interactions with us. Therefore, it is essential to evaluate these perspectives and decide which ones are relevant to our own understanding.

Ultimately, the role of others' views in self-discovery is to provide additional layers of insight .

Having self-awareness and understanding the context of our lives can be incredibly helpful. Others can challenge our beliefs, provide us with different perspectives, and help us to refine our self-image. However, the ultimate authority in understanding ourselves lies within us. We must take the external insights we receive and combine them with our own introspection to gain a full comprehension of who we are.

Embrace who you are and avoid comparison

Embracing who you are and not comparing yourself to others are both essential for fostering self-acceptance and personal growth. When you focus on your own unique qualities, strengths, and weaknesses, you create a strong foundation for genuine self-confidence and contentment. Comparing yourself to others can lead to feelings of inadequacy, jealousy, and insecurity, which can overshadow your own accomplishments and progress.

Everyone's journey is different, and no two paths are the same. Embracing who you are means acknowledging your strengths and weaknesses without judgment, and understanding that your worth isn't based on how you measure up to others. It's about recognizing that your uniqueness is what makes you valuable.

Comparison, on the other hand, can damage your sense of self by focusing on external factors. When you avoid comparing yourself to others, you open up the possibility for personal growth and self-discovery. Instead of chasing unrealistic standards, you can focus on your own goals and aspirations, which will help you to develop a healthier sense of accomplishment.

Remember, life is a continuous journey of self-improvement, and embracing yourself while avoiding comparison allows you to appreciate your progress, cultivate self-love, and lead a more fulfilling and authentic life.

Chapter Three

Negative mindset: A cage

Introduction to Negative Mindset

Negative thinking can be likened to a prison, trapping us in our own self-imposed boundaries and warping our view of the world. It is a state of mind where doubt, self-criticism, and a distorted view of reality take root. In this article, we will explore the complexities of a negative mindset – its sources, its effects, and its profound influence on our lives. By understanding the depths of this mental entrapment, we can start to break free from it, finding ways to cultivate a more empowered and hopeful outlook.

Causes of Negative Mindset

It's certainly understandable to have a negative mindset, and here's a breakdown of the causes. To start, there are internal factors like past experiences, self-doubt, and perfectionism. Then, there are external factors like negative influences, life circumstances, and social comparison. Additionally, cognitive distortions like all-or-nothing thinking, catastrophizing, and personalization can contribute to a negative mindset. Furthermore, fear of rejection and failure, lack of mindfulness and self-awareness, and avoidance behavior can all play a role. To sum up, these causes are interconnected and it's important to recognize and address them in order to overcome a negative mindset. Feel free to adjust this outline to fit your purpose or audience.

Effects of Negative Mindset

It is clear that a negative mindset can have a profound impact on individuals and families. It is important to understand the effects of this mindset on both individuals and family dynamics.

On an individual level, a negative mindset can lead to increased stress and anxiety, difficulty experiencing joy and positive emotions, diminished self-confidence, feelings of inadequacy and worthlessness, weakened immune system, sleep disturbances and fatigue, impaired decision-making abilities, difficulty concentrating and focusing, and negative impact on memory and learning. It can also lead to strained interactions, isolation, and a tendency to attract or maintain toxic relationships.

On a family level, a negative mindset can lead to communication challenges, such as focusing on problems and conflicts, limited positive communication, and misunderstandings due to negative interpretations. It can also have an impact on parent-child relationships, such as role modeling negative behavior and thought patterns, and strain on parent-child bonding and connection. In partner relationships, it can lead to increased conflicts and misunderstandings, erosion of intimacy and emotional connection, and an inability to support each other's personal growth. Finally, it can lead to a tense and negative environment, diminished sense of harmony and unity, and inhibition of shared positive experiences and memories.

The individual and family effects of a negative mindset are intertwined, creating a feedback loop where individual negativity contributes to family dynamics and family dynamics reinforces individual negativity. This can make it difficult to provide emotional support to negative individuals and to break free from a collective negative mindset.

In conclusion, it is important to be aware of the far-reaching consequences of a negative mindset and to take steps to overcome it and foster well-being in individuals and families.

Self-Limiting Beliefs

Here are 40 examples of self-limiting beliefs that can contribute to negative mindsets:

1. Perfectionism: Believing that nothing is worth doing unless it's done perfectly.
2. Fear of Failure: Thinking that failure defines your worth and is something to be avoided at all costs.
3. All-or-Nothing Thinking: Seeing situations as either perfect or a complete failure, with no middle ground.
4. Impostor Syndrome: Feeling like a fraud and doubting your accomplishments.
5. Comparison: Constantly comparing yourself to others and feeling inferior as a result.

6. Need for Approval: Believing you must always please others to be valued.

7. Catastrophizing: Assuming the worst possible outcome in any situation.

8. Victim Mentality: Feeling powerless and blaming external circumstances for your problems.

9. Fixed Mindset: Believing your abilities and intelligence are static and cannot be improved.

10. Labeling: Assigning negative labels to yourself based on past mistakes.

11. Overgeneralization: Drawing broad negative conclusions from isolated incidents.

12. Ignoring Strengths: Focusing solely on weaknesses and ignoring your strengths.

13. Limited Resources: Believing there's not enough to go around, leading to scarcity thinking.

14. Self-Sabotage: Subconsciously undermining your own efforts to avoid success or happiness.

15. Avoiding Risks: Staying within your comfort zone to avoid potential failure or discomfort.

16. Fearing Rejection: Assuming people will reject you, so you avoid initiating connections.

17. Belief in Fate: Thinking your life is predetermined, leading to lack of agency.

18. Money Mindset: Believing that money is the root of all problems or that you're undeserving of wealth.

19. Aging Anxiety: Feeling like opportunities decline with age.

20. Gender Roles: Believing certain tasks or roles are reserved for specific genders.

21. Inherited Limitations: Assuming you're bound by family history or circumstances.

22. Confirmation Bias: Only seeing evidence that confirms your negative beliefs.

23. Dependency: Relying excessively on others for your happiness or well-being.

24. Unrealistic Standards: Setting impossibly high standards for yourself in all areas of life.

25. Lack of Control: Feeling helpless in the face of life's challenges.

26. Rigid Identity: Identifying too strongly with a certain role and being resistant to change.

27. Mind Reading: Assuming you know what others think about you without evidence.

28. Social Expectations: Feeling obligated to meet societal norms even if they don't align with your desires.

29. Past Define Present: Believing your past mistakes define your current self and future potential.

30. Limited Learning: Thinking that learning stops after formal education.

31. Not Enough Time: Believing there's not enough time to pursue your passions or dreams.

32. Physical Appearance: Letting negative body image impact your self-esteem.

33. Defensive Pessimism: Always preparing for the worst to avoid disappointment.

34. Inferior Talents: Believing you lack talent compared to others.

35. Indecisiveness: Struggling to make decisions due to fear of making the wrong choice.

36. Lack of Support: Feeling alone and unsupported, even when there are people who care.

37. Holding Grudges: Letting past conflicts define your current relationships and interactions.

38. Fixed Circumstances: Believing your circumstances are unchangeable, even when they're not.

39. Diminished Creativity: Thinking you're not creative or imaginative.

40. Emotional Suppression: Believing that showing emotions is a sign of weakness.

These beliefs can lead to negative mindsets and impact your overall well-being. Recognizing and challenging them is a crucial step towards cultivating a more positive and growth-oriented mindset.

Overcoming Negative Mindset

Overcoming a negative mindset is not easy, but it is possible. Here is a guide to help you get started:

1. Awareness: Acknowledge and recognize your negative thoughts and beliefs. This is the first step to making a change.

2. Challenge Negative Thoughts: Analyze the accuracy of your negative thoughts. Ask yourself if they are based on facts or assumptions.

3. Reframe: Replace negative thoughts with more balanced and positive ones. Find evidence that contradicts your negative beliefs.

4. Practice Self-Compassion: Treat yourself with kindness and understanding, just as

you would a friend. Don't be too hard on yourself.

5. Mindfulness and Meditation: Practice mindfulness to stay present and observe your thoughts without judgment. Meditation can help calm your mind.

6. Gratitude Practice: Make a list of things you're grateful for regularly. Focusing on the positive aspects of your life can shift your perspective.

7. Set Realistic Goals: Break down larger goals into smaller, achievable steps. Celebrate your progress along the way.

8. Limit Social Comparison: Focus on your own progress rather than comparing yourself to others. Everyone's journey is unique.

9. Surround Yourself Positively: Spend time with people who uplift you and support your growth.

10. Physical Activity: Regular exercise can boost your mood by releasing endorphins and reducing stress.

11. Healthy Lifestyle: Eat well, get enough sleep, and avoid excessive alcohol or substance use. Physical well-being affects mental health.

12. Challenge Comfort Zones: Gradually step out of your comfort zone to build confidence and overcome fears.

13. Practice Resilience: View setbacks as opportunities for growth. Learn from failures instead of letting them define you.

14. Positive Affirmations: Use affirmations to challenge negative self-talk and reinforce positive beliefs.

15. Seek Professional Help: If your negative mindset is overwhelming, consider seeking help from a therapist or counselor.

16. Journaling: Write down your thoughts and feelings. This can help you process emotions and gain clarity.

17. Visualization: Imagine yourself succeeding and feeling positive. Visualization can help rewire your brain for optimism.

18. Limit Negative Inputs: Reduce exposure to negative news, social media, and other sources of negativity.

19. Learn from Mistakes: Instead of dwelling on failures, focus on what you've learned and how you can improve.

20. Practice Humor: Find humor in situations and don't take yourself too seriously.

21. Engage in Hobbies: Spend time doing things you enjoy. Hobbies can provide a sense of accomplishment and joy.

22. Help Others: Acts of kindness and helping others can boost your own sense of well-being.

23. Cognitive Behavioral Therapy (CBT): Consider CBT techniques to restructure negative thought patterns.

Remember, changing a negative mindset is a gradual process. Be patient with yourself and celebrate each small victory along the way.

Cultivating Resilience

Developing resilience is a valuable ability that gives you the strength and flexibility to manage life's difficulties. Here is a guide to help you cultivate resilience:

1. Positive Attitude: Foster an optimistic outlook. Concentrate on the possibilities within difficulties instead of focusing on the negatives.

2. Self-Awareness: Recognize your emotions and reactions. Be aware of how you respond to stressors.

3. Acceptance of Change: Welcome change as a natural part of life. Adaptability is essential to resilience.

4. Strong Social Support: Build healthy relationships. Rely on friends, family, or support networks during difficult times.

5. Problem Solving: Approach challenges as puzzles to solve. Break down issues into manageable pieces.

6. Effective Communication: Express your feelings and needs to others. Effective communication creates connections.

7. Healthy Coping Strategies: Use healthy methods to manage stress, such as exercise, meditation, and creative outlets.

8. Learn from Setbacks: View failures as opportunities to learn and grow. Resilience is built on the lessons of adversity.

9. Maintain Perspective: Keep challenges in perspective. Ask yourself, "Will this matter in a month, a year?"

10. Set Realistic Goals: Divide larger goals into smaller, achievable steps. Progress fuels resilience.

11. Self-Care: Prioritize your well-being. Sleep, nutrition, and relaxation directly affect your ability to bounce back.

12. Seek Professional Help: If needed, don't hesitate to consult therapists or counselors for guidance.

13. Cultivate Gratitude: Focus on what you have rather than what you lack. Gratitude increases resilience.

14. Practice Mindfulness: Stay present in the moment. Mindfulness reduces stress and strengthens resilience.

15. Learn to Say No: Prioritize tasks and commitments. Saying no when necessary preserves your energy.

16. Positive Relationships: Surround yourself with supportive people who promote growth and positivity.

17. Build Confidence: Remind yourself of past accomplishments. Self-assurance bolsters resilience.

18. Embrace Failure as Learning: Change your mindset from "failure" to "learning experience."

19. Face Fears Gradually: Confront fears in manageable steps. This gradually builds your capacity to face challenges.

20. Develop Flexibility: Be open to new approaches and viewpoints. Rigidity impedes resilience.

21. Keep Learning: Acquire new skills and knowledge. Learning encourages adaptability and resourcefulness.

22. Visualize Success: Imagine overcoming obstacles and achieving success. Visualization boosts resilience.

23. Help Others: Offering support to others can strengthen your own resilience and sense of purpose.

24. Practice Patience: Resilience takes time to build. Be patient with yourself as you learn and grow.

25. Celebrate Progress: Acknowledge small achievements on your resilience journey.

Remember that resilience is not about avoiding difficulties but facing them with a mindset that allows you to learn, adapt, and become stronger. It's a skill that you can continuously develop and refine over time.

Building Self-Esteem

Constructing self-esteem is a critical journey to a healthier and more positive self-image. Here's a guide to help you build and nurture your self-esteem:

1. Self-Reflection: Take the time to get to
know yourself better. Think about your
strengths, values, and accomplishments.

2. Positive Self-Talk: Replace self-criticism
with self-compassion. Challenge negative
thoughts and replace them with supportive
ones.

3. Set Realistic Goals: Break down larger
goals into achievable steps. Even small
successes can boost your self-esteem.

4. Celebrate Successes: Acknowledge your
accomplishments, no matter how small.
Celebrate your progress.

5. Practice Self-Care: Make sure to prioritize
your physical, emotional, and mental
well-being. Taking care of yourself sends a
positive message.

6. Healthy Boundaries: Set and maintain healthy boundaries with others. This shows respect for yourself and others.

7. Accept Imperfections: Embrace your flaws as part of your uniqueness. No one is perfect, and imperfections make us human.

8. Surround Yourself with Positivity: Spend time with people who uplift and support you. Avoid those who bring you down.

9. Mindfulness and Meditation: Practice mindfulness to stay present and reduce self-criticism. Meditation can boost self-awareness.

10. Learn New Skills: Acquiring new knowledge or skills enhances your sense of accomplishment and self-worth.

11. Face Challenges: Embrace challenges as opportunities for growth. Overcoming obstacles boosts self-esteem.

12. Visualize Success: Imagine yourself succeeding and feeling confident. Visualization can reinforce positive beliefs.

13. Accept Compliments: Learn to graciously accept compliments. Internalize positive feedback.

14. Practice Gratitude: Regularly acknowledge the things you're grateful for. Gratitude fosters a positive mindset.

15. Express Yourself Creatively: Engage in creative activities that allow you to express yourself freely.

16. Help Others: Acts of kindness and support for others can elevate your own self-esteem.

17. Limit Negative Influences: Minimize exposure to negative media, social media, and toxic relationships.

18. Healthy Lifestyle: Eat well, exercise, and get enough sleep. Physical well-being positively impacts self-esteem.

19. Challenge Comfort Zones: Step out of your comfort zone to prove to yourself that you're capable of growth.

20. Learn from Mistakes: View mistakes as learning experiences. Self-esteem grows from embracing failures as opportunities.

21. Engage in Positive Affirmations: Repeat positive statements about yourself regularly.

22. Build Competence: Continuously improve your skills and knowledge. Competence fuels self-esteem.

23. Help Yourself First: Prioritize your needs without feeling guilty. You deserve care and attention.

24. Practice Assertiveness: Express your needs and opinions with confidence. This reinforces your self-worth.

25. Forgive Yourself: Let go of past mistakes. Forgiveness is a step towards self-acceptance.

Building self-esteem is an ongoing process that requires patience and self-compassion. Be kind to yourself, and remember that your worth is not determined by external factors. Your belief in your own value is what truly matters.

Chapter Four

How long it takes to change

Factors Influencing Change Timeframe

It is clear that there are many factors that can influence the amount of time it takes to bring about change. These include the complexity of the change, the magnitude of the change, individual characteristics, motivation and readiness for change, external support and resources, commitment and consistency, personal beliefs and values, environmental factors, resistance to change, previous experiences, level of flexibility, degree of control, external pressures and deadlines, communication and education, availability of feedback loops, access to information, leadership and role models, and organizational structure. Knowing about these factors can help people, organizations, and leaders make informed decisions when implementing changes and anticipate the timeframes needed for successful transformation.

Personal Habits and Behaviors

The timeline for forming new habits or altering existing behaviors can differ greatly from person to person and is affected by a variety of factors. The "21-day rule," which suggests that it takes 21 days to form a new habit, is a popular belief, but research indicates that the time required can be longer and more complex.

This "21-day rule" originated from a study by plastic surgeon Dr. Maxwell Maltz in the 1960s. He noticed that it took about 21 days for his patients to adjust to changes in their appearance after surgeries. However, this observation was not based on thorough scientific research and has been misinterpreted over time.

Recent studies suggest that the time it takes to form a new habit or change a behavior can vary significantly and is more likely to be within the range of 18 to 254 days. A study conducted at the University College London found that on average, it takes about 66 days for a new behavior to become automatic, but this range can vary depending on the complexity of the behavior and the individual's characteristics.

There are several factors that influence how long it takes to form new habits or change behaviors:

1. Complexity of Behavior: Simple habits like drinking water after waking up may take less time to form than more complex behaviors like regular exercise.

2. Individual Differences: People differ in their level of motivation, willpower, and ability to adapt to change. Some individuals may be more naturally inclined to adopt new habits quickly.

3. Consistency: The more consistently a behavior is performed, the more likely it is to become a habit. Missing days can prolong the habit-forming process.

4. Behavior Type: Behaviors that provide immediate rewards are more likely to be adopted quickly. Habits with delayed or distant rewards might take longer to form.

5. Environmental Cues: Consistent cues or triggers in the environment can speed up habit formation.

6. Support and Accountability: Having a support system or being held accountable can accelerate the adoption of new behaviors.

7. Motivation and Willpower: High levels of motivation and willpower can speed up the habit-forming process.

8. Past Experiences: Previous successes or failures in habit formation can influence how quickly a new habit is established.

9. Routine: Incorporating the new behavior into an existing routine can aid in habit formation.

10. Mindfulness and Self-Awareness: Being mindful and aware of one's actions can hasten the process of habit adoption.

To sum up, while the "21-day rule" is an attractive concept, forming new habits or changing behaviors is a complex process that can take anywhere from a few weeks to several months. The key is consistency, perseverance, and understanding that individual experiences will vary. Setting realistic expectations and focusing on the long-term benefits of the habit change are essential for success.

Lifestyle Changes

The amount of time it takes to make major lifestyle changes can vary greatly depending on the type of change, the individual's readiness and motivation, the complexity of the adjustment, and the level of commitment. Let's take a look at some of the factors that can influence the timeline for implementing significant lifestyle changes:

1. Nature of the Change:
   - The type of lifestyle change is a major factor in how long it takes. Some changes, like changing dietary habits, may be implemented more quickly than more complex changes such as transitioning to a new career.

2. Readiness and Motivation:
   - People who are highly motivated and ready to make the change may be able to do so more quickly. Motivation is essential for taking the first steps and sustaining progress.

3. Commitment and Consistency:
   - Consistency is key to making lifestyle changes stick. Changes that are maintained over time are more likely to become part of one's daily life.

4. Gradual vs. Abrupt Changes:
   - Gradually introducing changes can be a more sustainable approach. Abrupt changes may lead to initial success but may be difficult to maintain in the long run.

5. Support and Resources:
   - Having a support system, access to resources, and relevant information can help speed up the implementation process.

Support networks provide encouragement and accountability.

6. Behavioral Complexity:
  - The complexity of the behavior being changed matters. Quitting smoking, for example, involves overcoming addiction and may take longer than adopting a new fitness routine.

7. Transition Period:
  - Major lifestyle changes often involve a transition period where old habits are gradually replaced with new ones. This period can vary based on individual progress.

8. Learning Curve:
  - Changes that require learning new skills or acquiring knowledge, such as adopting a new diet, can take longer as individuals adjust to the learning curve.

9. Psychological Adjustment:

- Significant lifestyle changes often require psychological adjustment. Individuals need time to adapt to the emotional and mental aspects of the change.

10. External Factors:
    - External factors such as family dynamics, financial constraints, or time availability can affect the pace of change.

11. Career Transition:
    - Transitioning to a different career can be a complex process that involves job searching, networking, acquiring new skills, and adjusting to a new work environment. This process can take several months to a year or more.

12. Dietary Changes:
    - Adopting a new diet involves learning about nutritional needs, planning meals, and changing shopping and cooking habits. It may take a few weeks to a few months to fully adjust.

13. Quitting Smoking:
   - Quitting smoking is a challenging
behavioral change due to addiction. While
the initial decision to quit can be immediate,
the process of overcoming cravings and
managing withdrawal can take several
weeks to months.

In summary, the timeframe for
implementing significant lifestyle changes is
highly individualized and influenced by
many factors. Setting realistic expectations,
seeking support, staying committed, and
taking a gradual approach can help ensure
successful adoption of lasting changes. It's
important to remember that change is a
process, and patience is key as individuals
work towards their goals.

Change Resistance and Persistence

Making changes can be a long and difficult process due to various factors such as resistance, setbacks, and unforeseen challenges. These can impede progress and create roadblocks in the process. Let's explore why this happens and discuss strategies for staying persistent:

1. Resistance to Change:
   - People often resist change out of fear of the unknown, comfort with familiar routines, or uncertainty about outcomes. This can slow down the process of change.

2. Setbacks and Obstacles:
   - Setbacks, unexpected challenges, or failures along the way can be demotivating. They may require additional time to overcome and resume progress.

3. Lack of Immediate Results:

- When individuals don't see immediate results, they may become discouraged. The absence of quick rewards can lead to frustration and a longer time commitment.

4. Complexity of Change:
   - Some changes involve complex behaviors, ingrained habits, or deep-seated beliefs. Overcoming these complexities takes time and effort.

5. Unrealistic Expectations:
   - Unrealistic expectations can lead to disappointment and feelings of failure. When change doesn't happen as quickly as anticipated, persistence can waver.

To stay persistent, here are some strategies to consider:

1. Set Realistic Expectations:
   - Acknowledge that change takes time and is rarely a linear process. Set achievable goals and be prepared for challenges.

2. Break Down Goals:
   - Divide larger goals into smaller, manageable steps. Each step accomplished boosts motivation and a sense of progress.

3. Stay Flexible:
   - Be open to adjusting your approach when faced with setbacks. Flexibility helps you navigate unexpected challenges more effectively.

4. Focus on Progress, Not Perfection:
   - Celebrate even small wins and steps forward. Remember that progress, no matter how incremental, is a positive sign.

5. Learn from Setbacks:
   - Instead of seeing setbacks as failures, view them as opportunities to learn and grow. Adjust your strategy based on what you've learned.

6. Seek Support:

- Reach out to friends, family, mentors, or support groups. Sharing your challenges and receiving encouragement can bolster persistence.

7. Visualize Success:
   - Imagine the end result and the positive impact the change will bring to your life. Visualization can reignite motivation.

8. Maintain Self-Compassion:
   - Be kind to yourself during setbacks. Negative self-talk hinders progress, while self-compassion fosters resilience.

9. Practice Patience:
   - Patience is vital in times of resistance or slow progress. Trust the process and stay committed.

10. Learn New Strategies:
   - If a particular approach isn't working, be willing to learn new strategies or seek professional guidance.

11. Reflect on Motivation:
   - Remind yourself why you wanted to make this change in the first place. Reconnecting with your motivations can reignite determination.

12. Keep a Progress Journal:
   - Document your journey, including successes, challenges, and lessons learned. Reflecting on your progress can renew motivation.

13. Reward Yourself:
   - Celebrate milestones along the way with small rewards that keep you motivated and excited about your progress.

Remember that persistence is essential for successful change. Challenges are a normal part of the process, and the ability to navigate them with resilience ultimately leads to lasting transformation.

Case Studies

Certainly, here are some real-life examples of changes that happened quickly and those that took longer to achieve:

Changes That Happened Quickly:

1. Learning a Language:
   - Example: Acquiring basic conversational phrases in a new language during a two-week vacation.
   - Analysis: Rapid language acquisition can occur when individuals are immersed in a language-rich environment and motivated to communicate their needs and connect with locals.

2. Adopting a Healthier Diet:
   - Example: Switching to a plant-based diet within a few months.
   - Analysis: Making the transition to a healthier diet can happen quickly when

there's a strong motivation, access to resources, and a clear understanding of dietary choices.

3. Digital Detox:
   - Example: Taking a break from social media for a month.
   - Analysis: Detaching from technology and social media can provide immediate benefits like reduced stress, leading individuals to quickly notice positive changes in their mental well-being.

Changes That Took Longer to Achieve:

1. Weight Loss and Fitness Transformation:
   - Example: Shedding a significant amount of weight and building muscle over the course of a year.
   - Analysis: Achieving a major transformation in physical health requires sustained commitment to dietary changes, regular exercise, and overcoming plateaus.

2. Career Change:
   - Example: Moving from a career in marketing to becoming a licensed therapist.
   - Analysis: Career changes involve education, training, and potentially obtaining certifications or degrees, leading to a longer transition timeline.

3. Overcoming Social Anxiety:
   - Example: Progressively managing and reducing social anxiety over the span of a few years.
   - Analysis: Overcoming mental health challenges like social anxiety involves gradual exposure, therapy, and developing coping mechanisms. It takes time to rewire thought patterns and responses.

4. Cultural Adaptation:
   - Example: Adjusting to a new culture and way of life after moving to a foreign country, taking several years.
   - Analysis: Adapting to a new culture involves understanding social norms,

language, and integrating into a new
community. It takes time to fully embrace
and assimilate into a different way of life.

Generally speaking, changes that happen
quickly often involve adjustments that yield
immediate benefits or are driven by strong
motivation. Changes that take longer usually
require more comprehensive adjustments,
involve personal growth, and necessitate
overcoming challenges that cannot be
addressed in a short period. The complexity
of the change, the level of commitment, and
the need for habit formation all contribute
to the varying timelines.